Date Due

TWENTY-FIVE YEARS
OF AMERICAN AID
TO JEWS OVERSEAS

A Record of the Joint Distribution Committee

By JOSEPH C. HYMAN

SECRETARY AND EXECUTIVE DIRECTOR
AMERICAN JEWISH
JOINT DISTRIBUTION COMMITTEE

NEW YORK · 1939

First published as part of Volume 41 of the American Jewish Year Book
by the Jewish Publication Society of America. Revised for this edition.

Anniversary Edition
Printed in the United States of America

ACKNOWLEDGMENT

The writer wishes to make sincere acknowledgment of the splendid assistance rendered in the entire preparation of this manuscript by Mr. Nathan C. Belth and Miss Fanny R. Adlerstein.

CONTENTS

I. THE WAR, 1914–1918

From time immemorial neither the heroes nor the victims of war have all been in the ranks of the contending armies. Death does not stop at the front lines and heroes are not always in uniform. No better proof of this can be found than in the story of American Jewish efforts to help and rescue Jewish victims of war, poverty and persecution in overseas lands. It is a story that has its beginnings in the greatest war man has ever known. It winds through a dreadful and chaotic peace, through a period of rebuilding, and finally through a series of recurring political upheavals, which have ended in another major European conflict. It is a story of the past quarter of a century, carrying within itself the thread of Jewish history.

American Jewish overseas relief efforts were born of an emergency and for the greater part of the past twenty-five years carried on in a spirit of emergency. Such has been the background of the agency established to cope with the problem—the American Jewish Joint Distribution Committee, generally referred to as the J. D. C. or the "Joint." Several times in its history, the Joint Distribution Committee has thought in terms of eventually disbanding, or of materially reducing its activity, believing that the emergency which had brought it into being or made its continuance necessary, had subsided. But each time there rose a new need, a new emergency which made it imperative for the Joint Distribution Committee to go on.

The history of the Joint Distribution Committee divides naturally into five chapters. The first is concerned with the World War period (1914-18) when Jews suffered not only from ravages of war visited upon all peoples caught between the contending armies, but from additional disabilities resulting from their unfavorable political and economic positions. There followed the post-war emergency relief period (1919-21), a time horrible in its suffering for Jews in Eastern Europe, perhaps more chaotic and dreadful for the civilian populations even than the war years. To an organization such as the Joint Distribution Committee, the almost complete disintegration of political, economic and social institutions brought unprecedented problems, and it became necessary to establish new machinery for the administration of relief.

In time this emergency subsided; out of the chaos came some order, and the Joint Distribution Committee began to devote itself to the problems of rehabilitation, of rebuilding. This is the third chapter—1921 to 1925. The organization was revamped along functional, reconstructive lines. Self-help agencies were formed in various countries and localities and encouraged to take over the work inaugurated by American Jews. Special foundations with specific reconstructive tasks were organized. The accent was on rebuilding and on self-help.

Eventually, it was felt, the Jews of the war-scarred communities would once more become self-supporting, and the Joint Distribution Committee—the agency that had been born of an emergency—might be able to retire from the field. That eventuality was near, it was thought, in 1925. But in the fall of that year, economic blight hit Poland and other East European lands. The Joint Distribution Committee could not liquidate lest the entire European Jewish structure of economic aid and welfare service which it had built up, collapse. Its support on a substantial scale continued through the years into the '30s, but constantly in the minds of American Jewish leaders was the hope that eventually economic and political conditions overseas might become such that the Jews of Eastern Europe would be enabled completely to attain self-support.

That was the situation in 1933, when Jewish life in Europe suffered the worst blow of all with the rise of the National Socialist regime to power in Germany. The events which have brought nearly all of the Jews in Europe into the shadow of disaster cast by spreading totalitarianism and the European war which broke out in September 1939, are contemporary history. As the Joint Distribution Committee completes its twenty-fifth year of existence, it is faced with problems even more staggering than those which prompted its inception. The end of this chapter is yet to be written.

The shot that killed the Austrian Archduke Francis at Sarajevo on June 28, 1914, brought Europe to the brink of war. In America it caused uneasy stirrings. Exactly a month later, Austria's armies marched into Serbia and after four days of threats and ultimata Russian troops invaded Germany and Germany invaded France. Before the month of August was over, Tannenberg, on the Eastern Front, had been won and lost.

And before the same fateful month of August had run its course, American Jews had received and answered the first plea for help from their co-religionists in the embattled territories. From Palestine, then under Turkish jurisdiction, there came to Louis Marshall and Jacob H. Schiff, leading members of the American Jewish Committee, an urgent cable from United States Ambassador Henry Morgenthau pleading that $50,000 be sent at once to save from actual starvation the 60,-

9

ooo Jews of Palestine who had been cut off by the warring armies. There followed appeals from responsible Jewish organizations in every belligerent country, but in the United States there was no single Jewish group able to meet this situation. Intensive organization, widespread fund-raising efforts were obviously needed.

The first attempt to form a general committee to meet the war emergency was made by the Union of Orthodox Congregations when on October 4, 1914, it organized the Central Relief Committee for the Relief of Jews, under the chairmanship of Leon Kamaiky. A few days later the American Jewish Committee called a conference of all Jewish organizations. Out of this came the American Jewish Relief Committee with Louis Marshall as president, Felix M. Warburg as treasurer, Cyrus L. Sulzberger as secretary, and David M. Bressler as assistant secretary. A public statement of policy was issued:

"Representatives of the leading national Jewish organizations and of the important Jewish communities of America have formed a general committee for the relief of the Jews, of the several European nations and of Palestine, who now or may hereafter require aid, in direct or in indirect consequences of the war. All Jews of every shade of thought, irrespective of the land of their birth, are solemnly admonished to contribute with the utmost generosity to the fund which must be gathered to meet this superlative need. The committee recognizes the economic distress which now bears heavily on all. That only emphasizes the obligation of making sacrifices and ennobles every gift the more.

"The fund collected is to be administered through such agencies as shall, in the judgment of the committee, best accomplish an effective and equitable distribution among those individuals and institutions whom it is sought to help, without waste or unjust discrimination. So far as it shall prove practicable the committee also proposes to receive and transmit funds from private individuals to their relatives abroad."

On November 22, 1914, the American Jewish Committee voted to transfer to the new Relief Committee the sum of $100,000 as a special emergency trust fund. It was obvious, however, that although both the Central Relief Committee and the American Jewish Relief Committee were well able to call upon two of the major sections of the Jewish population for funds, efficiency called for a single distributing agency of these funds. Five days later, therefore, the two relief committees joined in establishing the Joint Distribution Committee for the Relief of Jewish War Sufferers, with Felix M. Warburg as chairman. Within a few months a third fund-raising agency, designed to reach Jewish labor groups, was organized as the People's Relief Committee, with Meyer London as chairman. This group, too, became a constituent member of the Joint Distribution Committee.

The three committees had collected, by December 1915, over one and one-half million dollars. Toward the end of 1915 it became evident that concerted fund-raising efforts would be necessary. Led by Nathan Straus, who started with a contribution of $100,000, a drive was organized. A series of mass meetings were held, beginning with one in Carnegie Hall in New York on December 21, 1915. Impetus was given the fund-raising by a proclamation issued by President Wilson designating January 27, 1916, as Jewish Relief Day, in accordance with a resolution of the United States Senate. It was estimated that on this day alone over a million dollars was collected. By 1917 the fund-raising activities were organized on a community basis with each community accepting a quota in a nation-wide $10,000,000 campaign.

Through the efforts of Jacob Billikopf, who had been called upon to direct the campaign, a new standard of giving was set with a gift of $1,000,000 by Julius Rosenwald, made with the proviso that an additional $9,000,000 be raised during 1917. The inspired example set by Mr. Rosenwald was emulated throughout the country. In New York City, which had set itself a $5,000,000 goal, outstanding campaign work was done by Felix M. Warburg, David M. Bressler, I. Edwin Goldwasser and others. New York attained its quota after a ten-day campaign.

The task thus undertaken by the American Jewish community was complicated not only by the terrors of war, but by extraordinarily difficult political and economic conditions under which more than nine million Jews—half of all the Jews of the world—had been living for centuries in Eastern Europe.

Against a background of political, civil and economic burdens, the outbreak of the World War was for the Jews living in Eastern Europe a far greater calamity than for the non-Jewish population, bitter as was the fate of the latter. The Jews suffered all the miseries of a population caught between contending armies. But the Jews of Russia, moreover, felt the whiplash of a Russian soldiery which took its cue from the official attitude toward the Jews; the Jews of Poland had heaped on top of that the antagonism and resentment of the Poles; and the Jews of Galicia and Bukowina suffered from the redoubled fury of invading Russian armies which regarded them not only as Jews but as foreign enemies.

Perhaps the worst sufferers among the Jewish civilian population were the victims of enforced evacuation from the regions in which military operations were taking place. In Russia, these expulsions were begun very early in the war. They increased in intensity and extent with every defeat of the Russians. Only the rapid invasion and occupation of Poland and Lithuania by German troops prevented the complete explusion of the 2,000,000 Jews in that war zone.

In those territories which the Germans invaded before expulsion orders could be carried out, the Jews obtained some relief from political persecution, but their economic situation became worse than ever, for they found themselves in the path of a war machine that destroyed as it went.

Critical as conditions were in Russia and Poland in those years, they did not approach the utter devastation and terrible suffering in Galicia and Bukowina. Six times between 1914 and 1917 Russian armies swept over the territory and six times they were beaten back by Austrian forces. Each invasion and each retreat brought death and desolation to the local population.

In their efforts to alleviate these conditions, American Jewish leaders found the task of organization at home comparatively easy, for the Jews of the United States and Canada responded wholeheartedly to the appeals for funds. But how was relief to be brought to the stricken millions caught in the war area? With the best of intentions, the Joint Distribution Committee might not have been able to deliver a single sack of flour or a single bundle of clothing to a destitute Jewish community, if the State Department of the United States and other officials of our government had not looked kindly upon these humanitarian efforts as in keeping with the best American tradition. With such help, and with the assistance of neutral governments, the work of relief was made possible. Whenever feasible, the Joint Distribution Committee looked to those responsible local Jewish organizations still serving in the war area for administering relief funds, for even with the aid of the State Department, the J. D. C. was able to send only two of its own workers into the field in the early years. In 1916 the State Department authorized the first J. D. C. commission to go to Europe, but only two of its members were able to enter the war zone.

The part played by the J. D. C. during the actual war period in Russian relief work differed considerably from that in the territories overrun by the German forces, in Austria-Hungary, and in Palestine. In the latter regions the ruined Jewish communities were almost entirely dependent upon relief coming from America. In Russia, however, the Jews at the very outbreak of the war, were able to establish an efficient organization and to collect relief funds of their own. Furthermore, the Russian Government felt itself bound to aid the Jewish community to solve the relief problem, for it realized that a great deal of the misery among Jews was a consequence of the tactics of the Russian military authorities. The cooperation of the J. D. C. in Russia was nevertheless of great importance, both materially and morally.

The Jewish communities in the German occupied territories did not have the benefit of any appreciable resources of their own. In Poland and the Baltic countries, the Juedische Hilfskomite of Berlin was able to contact numerous communal and special relief committees to which it distributed the funds made available by the J. D. C. At the peak of German occupation of former Russian territories, the Hilfskomite reached 252 cities and towns.

In Warsaw there still existed a Jewish communal organization of national scope to which the Hilfskomite was able to bring American funds. The J. D. C. was also able to send funds directly to this committee through the American consul at Warsaw.

In Austria-Hungary and the Austrian occupied territories,

the Israelitische Allianz zu Wien and cooperating committees in Budapest, Lemberg and Cracow struggled manfully with an overpowering situation. Two-thirds of the population were rendered homeless; the refugee problem grew day by day; disease was rampant; and the condition of only 20 percent of the population was livable even on the basis of the low standards prevailing in sections of the occupied zones.

The severance of friendly relations between Germany and the United States, and the subsequent entry of the United States into the war, naturally created new complications in the relief efforts of the J. D. C., for it was completely blocked from continuing its work in behalf of the Jews in the territories occupied by the Central Powers. In August 1917, however, the State Department granted permission for the establishment of an agency in neutral Holland for the distribution of J. D. C. funds.

II. THE POST-WAR YEARS

The World War was merely the first act in the tragedy of European Jewry. The second act followed the Armistice and contained the climax of the play, a climax of suffering and sorrow. The end of the war marked the beginning of two of the blackest years in Jewish history. The Jews bore the brunt of the confusion, the turmoil, the chaos which enveloped Eastern Europe. Famine visited Poland, Russia, Rumania, Hungary and the Baltic countries. Thousands died of starvation; more fell victim to pillaging bands, to fire and sword. In the Ukraine alone 200,000 men, women and children were murdered in pogroms.

The years 1919–20 were years of disintegration. The map of Europe was changed. Empires were dismembered, submerged nationalities came to the surface, clamoring for independence and eager to dominate as large areas and populations as possible.

In this period of readjustment, the Jews suffered because their political and civil emancipation in European countries had been too recent to bring about their complete amalgamation with the people among whom they lived. They were still regarded as aliens. Furthermore, the conception of the State as a political unit in which different racial and political elements could cooperate for the good of the population as a whole, was as yet too new to be generally accepted. It was not accepted at all in Rumania and Russia, and in Poland the leaders of the new nation found it difficult to think of Poland as a country in which a large portion of the population would be Jewish. Anti-Jewish disorders in Poland were a consequence. The London *Times* reported that during the single month of November 1918, excesses occurred in not less than 110 towns and villages.

In Rumania anti-Semitism was already an old established institution, but in 1919 it became a more serious matter than ever before because it affected additional large numbers of Jews living in Transylvania and Bukowina, which had formerly been part of Austria-Hungary, and in Bessarabia, which was formerly a part of Russia. Rumanian animosity against the Jews was further increased by the clauses in the Versailles Peace Treaty which provided that racial, linguistic and religious minorities in Rumania be accorded equal civil and political rights with the majorities.

In Hungary, where anti-Semitism had been little known before the war, the Jews immediately became the objects of merciless and calculated persecution. On the one hand reactionaries charged Jews with responsibility for the outbreak of revolution which followed the collapse of the monarchy; on the other, the revolutionists charged the Jews with being bourgeois counter-revolutionists. The formation of Count Karolyi's liberal government in March 1919, was the signal for anti-Jewish riots throughout the country. The subsequent rise of Bela Kun's Soviet Republic was an economic catastrophe for Hungarian Jewry and when it fell, more violence and boycott was the lot of the Jew.

In Germany and Austria, although mob violence rarely occurred, the situation was often critical, varying with the political and economic conditions. Conditions in Austria were aggravated by the presence of war refugees from Russia, Poland and the Baltic provinces. In Lithuania, Latvia and Estonia, the civil population was the prey of bands of marauders; Jews were naturally the chief victims.

The calamity for the Jews was only a part of the disaster which shook all of Europe at the time. General conditions in Europe were such that the United States Congress was moved to set up the American Relief Administration and to appropriate $100,000,000 for its relief work. A European Relief Commission was established in which were included representatives of the Y. M. C. A., the J. D. C., the Society of Friends, the Red Cross and other organizations.

In this period of stupendous misery, the J. D. C. became the most important factor in the lives of the war-seared Jewish communities. It became the agency whereby the Jews of America were able to bring succor to the Jewish communities of Eastern Europe. In 1919 and 1920 the J. D. C. began to send abroad its own agents and experts, headed by Dr. Julius Goldman and Dr. Boris D. Bogen, to direct and control the work. Two successive units of some forty trained workers—sanitation, child care and economic experts—wearing the American uniform with the authority of the U. S. Government, went overseas to conduct their relief work. Two of the forty, Professor Israel Friedlaender and Rabbi Bernard Cantor, were murdered by marauding guerrillas.

It was during this period, also, that a large proportion of the appropriations made by the Executive Committee of the J. D. C. in New York were distributed by non-Jewish agencies, principally by governmental, quasi-governmental, and other publicly recognized bodies, such as the American Relief Administration, the U. S. Food Administration Grain Corporation, the Y. M. C. A., the Siberian Prisoners' Repatriation

18

Fund, the Near East Relief Commission, the American and British Friends' Societies, the American Red Cross and the Polish Relief Committee of America.

The conversion of American funds into the local currencies of various countries offered many complications because of violently fluctuating rates of exchange and extreme instability. An elaborate system of checks and controls had to be set up in order to safeguard American relief funds, and as soon as it was possible, a detailed audit was made by Morris C. Troper of the firm of Loeb and Troper, of the immense volume of transactions—both relief and remittance—made during the emergency. Largely responsible for the organization and supervision of this phase of the work was Mrs. Harriet B. Lowenstein Goldstein, Comptroller of the J. D. C.

The end of 1920 marked the recession, except in Russia, of the emergency period. Reconstruction work was begun in earnest, but hindering this work was one major problem —left as a bequest by the emergency period—the refugee problem. From July, 1921 to April, 1923, the Committee on Refugees, organized by the J. D. C., assisted a total of 300,000 people to emigrate, to become repatriated, to readjust themselves. They were given life and hope anew, enabled once more to establish homes and families.

The work of reconstruction, gigantic in scope, was made possible only because the American Jewish community realized that vast sums would be needed to reestablish the Jewish communities of Eastern Europe. There was a magnificent response to the fund-raising appeals of the Joint Distribution Committee and its three constituent committees. In 1919 and 1920, $27,000,000 was raised; in the following three years, under the campaign leadership of David A. Brown, another $20,000,-000 was contributed to the J. D. C.

A new administrative system was set up in the fall of 1921, on the arrival of James N. Rosenberg in Europe to serve as chairman of the European Executive Council of the J. D. C., which had been organized at the end of 1920. Earlier, James H. Becker of Chicago had served as Director-General of the J. D. C.'s European work, following the retirement of Dr. Julius Goldman. Under Mr. Rosenberg, who devoted a year in a voluntary capacity to the task, the entire scheme of administration was revised. Dr. Bernhard Kahn, later to become chairman of the European Executive Council, was made head of the Refugee Department, and other changes were made. In addition, a Finance Department was created under the direction of David J. Schweitzer, later vice-chairman of the European Executive Council.

To further the work of rehabilitation, five functional sub-committees were organized by the Joint Distribution Committee, each to give its attention to a special branch of reconstruction. Medical-sanitary programs were successfully conducted, child care activities promoted, schools and cultural institutions reestablished, trade training organized, economic support given. In addition, a transmission bureau was established to enable Jews in America to extend assistance to their relatives in Europe.

The first of the five functional sub-committees, under the chairmanship of David M. Bressler, concerned itself with the problem of the refugees. By 1923 the complicated refugee situation had been reduced to the point where only 25,000 persons had still to be cared for. The following year, however, saw a recurrence of anti-Jewish outbreaks. Coupled with this was the enactment by the United States Congress of the present restrictive immigration law, closing the major haven for the remaining refugees, many of whom were stranded in the seaports of England, Germany, Rumania, France and Holland. Nearly 8,000 prospective immigrants in Russia, already in possession of American visas, found that they could not emigrate because the Russian quota was filled.

An Emergency Refugee Committee was organized by the J. D. C. in June 1924, to bring immediate relief to those stranded in the various seaports. The following year an agreement was reached whereby the Emergency Refugee Committee, the Jewish Colonization Association and Emigdirect formed a United Evacuation Committee, 80 percent of whose funds were derived from the Emergency Refugee Committee. The stranded immigrants and refugees were registered and gradually helped to reestablish themselves in such lands as Canada, South America and Palestine. By the end of 1926 the situation had been cleared up.

The second of the functional committees, the Cultural Committee, under the chairmanship of Dr. Cyrus Adler, was charged with the reorganization of the school and educational systems destroyed by the war. Even at the height of the war relief period, a goodly part of the sums allotted by the J. D. C. and intended for Polish relief was applied by the beneficiaries to the upkeep of their schools and cultural institutions. Nevertheless, the entire Jewish educational system of Eastern Europe was destroyed by the war and a practically new system of education had to be established.

Though it is difficult to measure the work of the Cultural Committee in physical terms, some inkling of its achievement can be obtained from the fact that it created and restored and helped maintain in Europe almost 1,800 educational institutions, ranging from elementary schools to academies of higher learning, with a total attendance of 225,000 students. In addition, the Cultural Committee gave special aid to rabbis, writers, teachers and spiritual leaders. It was a major factor in dissipating the demoralizing influences born of the war.

The task facing the third of the functional committees, the Medical and Sanitary Committee, with Bernard Flexner as chairman, was almost insurmountable. When a J. D. C. medical commission arrived in Poland in 1921, it found conditions of indescribable filth and disease. Up to that time the medical work was a part of the general relief program and was necessarily treated on an emergency basis. Typhus was reported in almost every community in Poland. Other epidemic diseases reached a critical stage in 1920 and during the early months of 1921. The famine, the exchange of refugees between Poland and Russia, and the consequent movements of large bodies of men, women and children, were factors in reviving the typhus epidemic in cities and towns bordering on those countries, and continually threatened a widespread epidemic in all districts of Volhynia, Brest-Litovsk and Bialystok.

There were virtually no bathing facilities. The old bathhouses were in ruins. Dispensaries were few; orphanages, homes for the aged and schools were unsanitary. There existed no adequately trained local personnel of physicians, dentists and nurses. Water supplies were almost invariably polluted; sewage and refuse disposal was of a most primitive nature. Those homes which survived the devastation of the war were generally unclean and vermin-infested. There were no active, well-organized relief organizations among the Jews in Poland, and the work of the government was too general and ineffectual. The great mass of the population was undernourished, poorly clothed, and deprived of elementary sanitary measures. Tuberculosis, notably of bones, joints and glands, was prevalent.

The Medical Commission planned to fight these conditions on two fronts. It felt that the problem of sanitation would have to be solved before normal conditions would return. These problems, however, required unlimited resources and essentially should have been the tasks of government agencies. Secondly, immediate medical relief involving the rebuilding, subsidizing and organization of medical institutions had to proceed at once. To this task the Medical Commission bent all its efforts.

Perhaps the most notable accomplishment of the J. D. C. in this field was the help it rendered in the organization and re-organization of small health societies, culminating in the organization of the Society for Safeguarding the Health of the Jews in Poland (Toz), through which the J. D. C. has since worked in carrying out the major part of its medical program in Poland. In similar fashion, for the other border countries, the J. D. C. subsidized and cooperated with the Oze, the Russian Jewish medical association which had played an important part in war relief work and now continued its ministrations. Another outstanding accomplishment was the foundation of the Nurses Training School in Warsaw, an institution whose achievements have been recognized by the League of Nations.

In Palestine, the J. D. C. established a Malaria Research Unit, which, working in conjunction with the Department of Health of the Palestine Government, performed vital pioneering work in the permanent elimination of breeding places of malaria. As a result, the Rockefeller Foundation sent another unit to Palestine to work with the first unit. The success of this work received widespread notice and recognition.

For a number of years, the J. D. C. Medical Committee also worked in close cooperation with the Zionist Organization of America and Hadassah in hospitalization and medical work in Palestine.

The fourth committee, charged with child care work, and headed by Dr. Solomon Lowenstein, also continued a function which stemmed from the war relief period, during which subventions were granted by the J. D. C. to child care institutions in Poland. At the close of the war, the number of orphans in Eastern Europe outside of Russia was estimated at 60,000. Perhaps 60 percent of these orphans had theretofore been provided for by the J. D. C. and almost 18,000 still remained under its care. In Palestine, the Orphans' Committee, supported largely by funds contributed by the J. D. C., cared for 1,300 children.

In the post-war years, the J. D. C. stimulated local communities in Poland and other countries in Eastern Europe to engage in child welfare work on a large scale. As a result, the J. D. C.'s war orphan work grew into general orphan work and then into general child care, embracing all types of social service for children. Summer colonies, trade schools, work shops and other institutions were established and fostered during this period. By 1925 rapid strides had been made by the Child Care Department in fostering local and central child care organization. In time, all the functions of child care in Poland were placed into the hands of a federation of these organizations—Centos.

The fifth and perhaps most far-reaching of the five functional committees, the Committee on Reconstruction, under the leadership of Herbert H. Lehman, was charged with the economic rehabilitation of the East European Jewish communities.

Three major activities stand out in the economic rehabilitation program of the J. D. C.: the creation, restoration and promotion of credit cooperatives and loan societies; assistance in the rebuilding of homes; and the repair, restoration and maintenance of trade and technical schools. The loan *kassa,* or cooperative, had been a well-established institution in Eastern Europe prior to the war. But with the collapse of economic life the entire network of these credit cooperatives was virtually wiped out.

The European Reconstruction Department, organized in 1921, made a series of surveys in Poland, Lithuania, Latvia and Hungary to determine the methods best adapted for economic reconstructive work in those countries. The reestablishment and strengthening of these cooperative societies to serve as instrumentalities for the rehabilitation of Jewish war sufferers, became the paramount objective of the Reconstruction Committee.

In time the functional committees developed a new type of machinery, through which the J. D. C. operates to this day. The burden of responsibility was passed on more and more to European Jews themselves, who administered their own affairs. Special organizations were formed to carry on the work of the Joint Distribution Committee. In 1924 most of the economic reconstruction work was transferred to the American Joint Reconstruction Foundation, organized by the Joint Distribution Committee and the Jewish Colonization Association. The Foundation created a large network of cooperative loan societies that are today an important economic factor in the lives of the Jews in Eastern Europe. The J. D. C.'s economic, industrial and farm development work in Palestine was turned over to the Palestine Economic Corporation in 1926.

In 1924, the work in Russia was turned over to the Agro-Joint (American Jewish Joint Agricultural Corporation), as the operating agency of the J. D. C. The medical work, the child care work, the trade-training work in Poland, Rumania, Lithuania and other sections of Eastern Europe, were turned over to local organizations. These have been and still are assisted by the Joint Distribution Committee, although the largest part of their budgets is covered by local contributions. The local institutions, whether work shop, hospital or loan society, bear no J. D. C. insignia. Yet there is scarcely an organization in Eastern Europe, but has been the beneficiary of American generosity through the J. D. C.

III. THE AGRO-JOINT IN RUSSIA

The work in Russia is a separate chapter in the history of the Joint Distribution Committee and a special field of its activities. As noted heretofore, the relations between the new government of Russia and the United States in the Fall of 1919 became strained. In the winter of that year and in 1920 the J. D. C. made urgent but futile efforts to institute relief work there. Great as was the misery of the Jewish people, it was impossible to organize any considerable relief activity prior to the year of the great famine—1921.

The catastrophic crop failure in 1921 meant mass starvation for the country; but the famine brought the American Relief Administration, under the direction of Herbert Hoover, into the field and this meant large-scale relief, not only for the general population, but also for the Jews of Russia. A conference of all American relief organizations was called in Washington by Mr. Hoover. Representing the J. D. C. were Felix M. Warburg, James N. Rosenberg and Lewis L. Strauss. Here the groundwork was laid for relief efforts in Russia. A contribution of $675,000 in food supplies was made by the J. D. C., and Dr. Boris D. Bogen and Dr. Joseph A. Rosen, representing the J. D. C., were sent to Russia with the American Relief Administration mission. In October 1921, an agreement was drawn in London whereby extensive relief work was undertaken in Southern and Western Russia where the bulk of the Jewish population lived. Mr. Strauss, who served as acting chairman of the J. D. C.'s Committee on

Russia at the invitation of its chairman, Louis Marshall, conferred with Mr. Hoover in Washington to effect an arrangement for these joint A. R. A.-J. D. C. feeding operations in the Ukraine and was instrumental in working out the program.

All of the relief activities of the J. D. C. in Russia at this time were part and parcel of the A. R. A. operations. The records show the largest number of children fed at any one time was 1,020,762, when the famine was at its height just prior to the harvest in 1922. Adult feeding in this period in the Ukraine reached the daily figure of 800,000 persons. During the famine a large non-sectarian student feeding program was supported by the Y. M. C. A. and the J. D. C.

Anticipating the withdrawal of the American Relief Administration from Soviet Russia, the J. D. C. entered into an agreement with the Soviet Government enabling it to continue to work independently. At this time, J. D. C. emergency relief activities outside of Russia had already been liquidated. In Russia, however, the emergency was still acute. The work there assumed a two-fold character. General relief was administered while reconstructive activities were developed.

During the period of independent relief and reconstructive operations, conducted directly by representatives of the J. D. C. in Russia, approximately $4,220,000 was appropriated. Ten tractor squads were formed, and with 85 tractors purchased in the United States, about 180,000 acres of land were plowed. Pure seed multiplication stations were established. Live stock was purchased and distributed. Foreign machinery and implements were furnished; wells were drilled; dairy cooperatives were organized. Houses were built and repaired in the devastated Jewish colonies.

Other reconstructive activities initiated by the J. D. C. included the revival of the artisan *kassas,* assistance to local Jewish mutual aid societies, subventions to hospitals, clinics, ambulatoria and medical societies, establishment of trade schools, and subsidies to homes for the aged, orphanages and other philanthropic institutions. The work thus inaugurated during the period of independent activities of the J. D. C was later continued by the Agro-Joint.

Medical work, too, was inaugurated by the J. D. C. and over 1,500,000 persons received treatment in the ambulatoria and hospitals subventioned by the J. D. C. Child welfare work received particular attention. The number of Jewish war and pogrom orphans in the Ukraine and White Russia was estimated at 300,000. Local Jewish organizations were able to care for about 100,000 of these children. The J. D. C. extended its relief work to at least 30,000 children in various institutions, transferring them into clean and livable quarters, providing the children with supplementary rations of food, with shoes, underwear, outer clothing and medical attention. The refugee problem, especially in the Ukraine, was grave. The big cities harbored scores of thousands of fugitives from smaller communities destroyed by pogroms. Here again the J. D. C. was able to do effective work in repatriating thousands to their native villages or settling them in new places.

The process of reconstructing Jewish life in Russia and re-orienting Jews to the changed conditions in the country, however, called for unusual measures beyond the general reconstructive program followed in the other countries of Eastern Europe. On July 21, 1924, therefore, the American Jewish Joint Agricultural Corporation (Agro-Joint) was organized by the J. D. C. as its operating agency in Russia.

The task before the Agro-Joint was so to restratify Jews in the economic field that they would be given citizenship and would receive equal rights with the privileged classes of workers and peasants. It was generally recognized that from the point of view of permanent rehabilitation, mass transition to productive occupations was the only solution to the problems confronting the Jews in Soviet Russia, who numbered at that time approximately 2,750,000.

The Agro-Joint began work with an experimental project for settling several hundred Jewish families on the soil. By the end of 1926 the results of this experiment had so far exceeded the most optimistic expectations of the Joint Distribution Committee that it was decided to continue this effort as a more extensive project. Dr. Joseph A. Rosen was appointed director of the Agro-Joint to carry out the land settlement program and a number of industrialization projects, which were all designed to redirect a substantial proportion of the Jewish population of Russia into agricultural and industrial occupations.

The Government was in full sympathy with the work of the Agro-Joint and, by supplying free land, reduced transportation rates, free tracts of timber, and financial credits, furnished the greater part of the necessary investment.

From 1924, when it began operations with an initial appropriation of $400,000 from the Joint Distribution Committee, till the end of 1928, the Agro-Joint expended approximately $5,880,000. In that year, the further financial support of the Agro-Joint work was taken over by the American Society for Jewish Farm Settlements in Russia, Inc., with James N. Rosenberg as chairman. The Society, led by Felix M. Warburg, Julius Rosenwald, James N. Rosenberg, Paul Baerwald, Herbert H. Lehman and Louis Marshall, without resorting to any general appeal, secured $8,000,000 in private subscriptions, payable over a period of eight years, from a small group of individuals in the United States. Notable in this connection was a $5,000,000 subscription by Julius Rosenwald. These sums were made available to the Agro-Joint for the extension of its work. By agreement with the Society and the Agro-Joint, the Government of the U. S. S. R. contributed in roubles an amount equal to the dollar payments of the Society toward the agricultural colonization and industrialization programs in Russia, and accorded other important facilities.

The Agro-Joint projects resulted in permanent improvements. The scope of the work included not only farm settlement, but industrialization, training and other activities for the Jews dwelling in the cities, small towns and villages. At certain stages of development in all the Agro-Joint projects, the work was taken in hand by local government agencies, fitted into the general structure of economic and social life of the country, and continued on a larger scale at the expense of the Government.

The land settlement work grew into a vast movement that settled 250,000 people on 3,000,000 acres of land in colonies in the Ukraine and the Crimea. By 1937 the collectives had become strong enough to take new members into the colonies without outside help, and to provide large funds for general improvements, electrification of villages, irrigation, water supply and other projects.

In cooperation with the Jewish Colonization Association (ICA), the Agro-Joint operated 300 loan societies for the financing of artisan cooperative projects. In 1937 these were absorbed into the general system of cooperatives financed by the Government Bank which enabled them to continue working on a scale larger than any social welfare organization would have been able to provide.

During the course of the years, the Agro-Joint also organized 42 trade and farm schools, some of them conducted with the partial cooperation of the ICA and the ORT. These schools trained thousands of young Jews who were thereafter placed in Government industries. Short courses were also conducted for adults. These institutions, too, were eventually absorbed by the Government Trusts and Departments and continued on a larger scale.

Another phase of this work was conducted through mutual aid societies with the support of the Agro-Joint. These societies organized cooperative shops which taught trades to tens of thousands of the "lishentzy"—the declassed—who were not suitable for farm settlement. Since 1935 these, too, have been gradually absorbed by local government industrial trusts or the regular system of cooperatives.

The Agro-Joint also carried on a vital service in the field of medical aid and public health. It organized 63 medical societies which waged successful fights against tuberculosis, trachoma, favus and other diseases which had ravaged the impoverished Jewish population.

The Agro-Joint began the process of winding up its activities in the Soviet Union late in 1937 and continued through 1938. This action was taken when it was found that Russian Jews no longer required the assistance of outside organizations.

Since the inception of the Agro-Joint in 1924, it had administered a total of approximately $16,000,000 for land settlement work, as well as industrialization, medical, trade school and mutual aid activities. This included the funds provided by the Society. Through an arrangement effected with the

Government of the U. S. S. R., the Society, in consideration of its investment in the agricultural settlement programs, received for the beneficial interest of subscribers, certain bonds from the Government of the U. S. S. R.

In less than a decade and a half, the work of the Agro-Joint helped to transform Russian Jewry from a downtrodden, almost helpless ghetto population into self-reliant and productive workers of the field and factory. It had liquidated the problem of the Jewish "lishentzy" or declassed group. Former President Herbert Hoover, who as director of the American Relief Administration had an opportunity to know the problem facing the Agro-Joint, called the Agro-Joint achievement, long before its conclusion, one of the most amazing feats of "human engineering" in modern history.

IV. THE AMERICAN JOINT RECONSTRUCTION FOUNDATION

In the meantime, the activities of the Reconstruction Committee in other countries of Eastern Europe had been assumed largely by the American Joint Reconstruction Foundation, which was established on May 3, 1924, by the Joint Distribution Committee and the Jewish Colonization Association (ICA). Sir Leonard Cohen, later succeeded by Sir Osmond d'Avigdor Goldsmid, became the chairman of the Foundation; Felix M. Warburg, and later Bernard Flexner, acted as American vice-chairmen. To the Foundation was turned over a large part of the task of reconstructing and improving the general economic conditions of the Jewish population in Poland and other countries by encouraging and facilitating economic reconstructive activity.

The most important phase of the work of the Foundation, and the one upon which it has concentrated throughout its history, is the credit cooperative movement. The effect of the credit cooperative has been to organize many individually weak forces into a strong financial unit and thus to provide a credit and banking structure for Jews who would in no other way be able to obtain credit for their economic activities. In the countries in which the Foundation operated there were, as of November, 1938, 687 credit cooperative societies or kassas affiliated with it, with a membership of 191,000 small businessmen, farmers and artisans.

The entire capital of the Foundation was contributed by

the J. D. C. and the ICA. The J. D. C. transferred to the Foundation at its inception all the outstanding assets of the Reconstruction Department. Through subsequent agreements between the J. D. C. and ICA, the resources of the Foundation were considerably increased, the J. D. C. contributing in all upwards of $3,000,000 and the ICA upwards of $2,000,000.

At the present time the Foundation operates in Bulgaria, Slovakia, Estonia, Finland, Greece, Latvia, Lithuania, Poland, four sections of Rumania and Turkey. Operations in Germany, which were begun in 1933, had to be liquidated under German regulations by December 31, 1938. Foundation activities in Austria were likewise liquidated. Loan funds were also made available for the aid of Jewish refugees from Germany in such countries as France, England, Holland, Palestine and the United States. From the inception of the Foundation in 1924, through November, 1938, kassas affiliated with it granted, out of their own capital and J. D. C. credits, in revolving funds, a total of 5,052,000 loans aggregating $581,-000,000.

Aside from the credit cooperatives, the Foundation contributed greatly to the economic upbuilding of the stricken and harassed Jewish populations of Eastern and Central Europe, through special loans to building cooperatives and cooperative bakeries, through long-term agricultural credits and other forms of basic economic assistance. Indispensable as the Foundation always was to the Jewish trader, the small merchant, the artisan and the agriculturist, as virtually the only source of cheap credits, it has become increasingly important, as recent years of economic depression, with their mounting waves of anti-Semitism, have sharply limited the few remaining business opportunities and occupations of large groups of the Jewish population.

The operations of the Foundation were conducted from the outset in accordance with efficient and approved cooperative principles and were necessarily designed to conserve for the members of the cooperatives, the shareholders and depositors, a well-secured, unimpaired revolving fund for continued service. The Foundation on numerous occasions, however, did not hesitate to assume large losses when the Jewish people were the special victims of regulations and statutes that worked unusual hardship upon them, and when aggravated and growing impoverishment and acute economic crisis made it virtually impossible for the borrowers to repay the cooperatives.

V. THE ECONOMIC CRISIS

With the establishment of the Agro-Joint and the American Joint Reconstruction Foundation as subsidiary agencies and the development of strong local organizations for medical work, child care, educational and other activities, the Joint Distribution Committee in 1925 considered the possibility of liquidating or of sharply reducing its own work. The J. D. C. had been born of emergency and it was felt that the emergency was nearing a close. However, a group of J. D. C. officers visited Eastern Europe and Russia to view conditions prior to taking action. They returned convinced that the time had not yet come for liquidation. They called instead for new efforts, for they found that the social structure which had been rebuilt from the ruins of the war would collapse if American support were withdrawn.

The economic crisis which was sweeping Poland in 1925 and continued through 1926 was paralyzing industry and commerce. Unemployment had assumed tremendous proportions. Of 212,000 Jewish workingmen in the entire country, half were out of work. Of 62,650 Jewish artisans more than 80 percent were idle. In Warsaw 83 percent of the Jewish workers were unemployed. In Bessarabia crop failures during two successive years resulted in famine. It was necessary to reinforce and strengthen all of the organized reconstructive, medical, child care and communal agencies.

In the fall of 1925, the findings of the group were presented to a national conference called by the J. D. C. Again the

J. D. C. appealed to the Jews of America for large funds and, as a result, on September 25 a United Jewish Campaign for $15,000,000 was launched, once more under the direction of David A. Brown, to provide for the needs in Russia, Eastern Europe and Palestine. Within the next five years, the J. D. C. was enabled to assure the continuation of its work on a large scale. By the end of that period, however, the world-wide economic depression had reached the United States and contributions fell off considerably.

With the campaign under way in 1926, the J. D. C. took two further steps to strengthen its efforts overseas. In the first place, it decided to turn over its assets and its work in Palestine to the newly formed Palestine Economic Corporation; and secondly, it took steps to supplement the economic activity of the cooperative loan societies and the Foundation in Poland by fostering free loan societies, Gemiloth Chesed kassas, which had been at one time well established institutions in Polish Jewish life. These kassas provided free credits for such small merchants, artisans and workers who were not able to avail themselves even of the low interest credit facilities of the cooperatives. In the course of the years, the J. D. C. invested well over $2,000,000 in these kassas and an equal sum was invested locally. The free loan societies grew in importance to the point where they even overshadowed the cooperatives. In the 1930's they came to occupy the key position in the economic life of the Jews of Poland.

The Palestine Economic Corporation was organized in February, 1926 and represented a merger of assets amounting to $1,800,000 held in Palestine by the Reconstruction Committee of the J. D. C. and the assets of the Palestine Cooperative Company. The J. D. C. had been able to liquidate or turn over to local organizations in Palestine its child care, medical

38

and other activities. It was felt that the work of helping to build a sound economic footing for Jews in Palestine must go forward.

To this task the Palestine Economic Corporation was dedicated. The Corporation, through its various subsidiaries, contributed to the growth of basic industries with substantial investments and made credits available to farmers, artisans, small merchants and manufacturers. The subsidiaries operated by the Corporation included a number organized by the J. D. C., such as the Central Bank of Cooperative Institutions and the Loan Bank, Ltd., which the J. D. C. continued to operate until 1932. Other subsidiaries include the Palestine Mortgage and Credit Bank, the Palestine Water Company, and the Bayside Land Corporation. The Corporation has also substantial investments in Palestine Potash, Ltd., Palestine Hotels, Palestine Foundries and Metal Works, Agricultural Mortgage Company and the Palestine Electric Corporation.

VI. THE NAZI ERA

By the end of 1932, at the completion of eighteen years of heroic labors, the J. D. C. had a record of expenditures totaling well over $80,000,000. It was during this year, too, that Paul Baerwald became chairman of the J. D. C. and Felix M. Warburg assumed the honorary chairmanship of the Committee. Mr. Baerwald had been prominent in the work of the J. D. C. since 1917, first as assistant treasurer, and later as treasurer. The world-wide economic crisis had made such inroads into the giving possibilities of American Jews that it was deemed inadvisable to conduct a full-fledged fund-raising campaign during 1932. While the Jews of Eastern and Central Europe were still tragic victims of the depression, and while sharp discrimination imposed further burdens on them, the J. D. C. had gone a long way toward accomplishing its ends. It had built up sturdy institutions of self-help in Eastern Europe and had helped to make local populations so conscious of their communal obligations as to furnish the bulk of the funds needed for programs of social and economic welfare. The monumental reconstructive task of the Agro-Joint in Russia was almost completed; the Palestine Economic Corporation had been organized and was able to stand on its own feet in promoting economic development in the Holy Land.

And then, in March of 1933, a new calamity engulfed Europe's Jews; Adolf Hitler became Chancellor of Germany. Within a few weeks, appeal after appeal came from the German Jewish community of some 600,000 souls. The Jews of

America, eager to rescue their co-religionists from the raging torrent of Nazism, clamored for some unified, organized and experienced channel whereby they might be of assistance. The Joint Distribution Committee, which had gained international recognition for its efficient aid in years of former crisis, which was known and respected by governments, and which had established the type of fund-raising machinery best calculated to reach every segment of America's Jews, was pressed into service to meet the new emergency.

During the summer and fall of 1933, a number of J. D. C. officers and colleagues visited Germany, the first of the group being Dr. Jonah B. Wise, who took an active part in the establishment of a central German Jewish welfare organization—the Zentral Ausschuss fuer Hilfe und Aufbau. A whirlwind campaign in the late summer and early fall of 1933, under Dr. Wise's leadership, resulted in subscriptions of $1,350,000 to meet the new emergency. Dr. Wise had been chairman of the campaign committee of the J. D. C. for several years.

From the outset, it was clear that the J. D. C. must adhere consistently to its traditional policy and limit its efforts solely to programs of relief and reconstruction. Questions affecting the legal, political and civic status of the Jews of Germany, and the safeguarding of their rights, were not within the province of the organization. The J. D. C., operating in direct relief programs in Germany and other lands, continued to engage in non-political and non-propaganda functions. In keeping also with the tradition that it must work through and with responsible local agencies, the J. D. C. began to make funds available through the Zentral Ausschuss for a program of emigration aid, economic aid, trade and vocational schooling and welfare service.

The first precipitate exodus of thousands of Jews from Germany was followed by the sobering conclusion, on the part of the German Jews themselves, that hundreds of thousands of them would perforce have to attempt to readjust their lives within Germany itself and train their youth for new callings in preparation for ultimate settlement in other lands. It was impossible, in 1934, to anticipate the tragic blows which fate still held in store for Germany's Jews.

The J. D. C., not content with undertaking to fulfill the responsibility of American Jews toward their suffering co-religionists in Germany, approached central Jewish organizations in England and France. It reached agreements with the Central British Fund for German Jewry in England, whereby certain parts of the relief program in Germany and of refugee aid and emigration assistance was subventioned in common. The Jewish Colonization Association likewise assumed a substantial share of responsibility toward the refugee problem.

The word "refugees" once more became a commonplace. Fleeing from the terrors of a private war, aimed at crushing out their very existence, thousands upon thousands of German Jews swarmed out of Germany, desperately seeking admission to any land which would have them. The problem of these helpless unfortunates soon became one of international and intergovernmental scope, and in December 1933, less than nine months following the accession to power of the Nazi Party, the League of Nations established a High Commission for Refugees, with Hon. James G. McDonald as the first High Commissioner.

At the very inception of the plans for the establishment of the High Commission, the J. D. C. placed its facilities and personnel at the disposal of Mr. McDonald and his cooperating agencies. It contributed substantially, not merely to the administrative budget of the High Commission, but also to the entire program of coordination and of aid which the High Commissioner attempted to institute.

Conscious of the obligations of American Jews to German refugees, not alone overseas but in the United States, where several thousand had already begun to arrive, the J. D. C. cooperated closely, during this period, in the establishment of the German Jewish Children's Aid, which was incorporated to make provision for such German children as could be brought to the United States, and of the National Coordinating Committee for Aid to Refugees and Emigrants Coming from Germany, which was intended to centralize all activities in behalf of German refugees in the United States. It also maintained contact with non-Jewish refugee organizations: The American Committee for Christian German Refugees, the Committee for Catholic Refugees from Germany, the American Friends' Service Committee, and other sectarian and interdenominational bodies.

By the end of 1933, the refugee problem had assumed such magnitude in European countries that it was necessary to mobilize local resources in such countries as France, Holland, Belgium, Switzerland, Czechoslovakia, Italy, Austria and Poland, in order to embark on a large program of aid for the destitute thousands seeking asylum. Where local resources were inadequate, the J. D. C. supplemented, within its means, the activities and programs of the local refugee aid organizations. The largest part of the funds for emigration were made available through the Hicem, which had been founded many years earlier through the joint efforts of the Jewish Colonization Association and the American HIAS. While these two agencies continued to provide the administrative costs of the Hicem, it was the J. D. C. which supplied, and has continued to furnish, the largest part of the actual transportation expenses of German Jewish emigrants assisted by the Hicem.

Subventions were also given, not alone to Jewish committees, but to such non-Jewish and non-sectarian bodies as the Society of Friends, International Student Service, International Committee for Securing Employment for Refugee Professional Workers, Emergency Committee in Aid of Displaced German Scholars, Emergency Committee in Aid of Displaced Foreign Physicians, and others.

In March 1934, it became apparent that the Jewish emergency in Germany would be of long duration and would require intensive aid on the part of American Jews. At the same time, there were recognized the advantages of eliminating competitive and duplicating fund-raising. Thus, under date of March 11, 1934, there was launched the $3,000,000 United Jewish Appeal for 1934, combining the campaigns of the Joint Distribution Committee and the American Palestine Campaign, the latter organization being the American representative of the Jewish Agency for Palestine.

Despite the overwhelming pressure of German needs, at no time did the J. D. C. fail to continue its vital work in Eastern Europe. Indeed, as the shadow of Nazism lengthened and totalitarian ideologies spread, the needs in Eastern Europe were intensified. Not only did a large number of repatriates to both Poland and Rumania from Germany swell the ranks of those requiring aid, but the repercussions of the intense anti-Semitic measures in Germany resulted in increased hardships for the weakened Jewish populations of East European countries. The cumulative effects of the general world depression had rendered the position of Poland's and Rumania's Jews critical; as minority peoples they not only shared the general and prevailing poverty of their non-Jewish neighbors, but were subject to special disabilities which aggravated their condition. In Poland, in 1934, as well as now, more than a million Jews lived below the subsistence level; starvation, poverty and disease took a terrific toll of their number. The growing strength and numbers of state monopolies, which displaced the Jews in many commercial and industrial fields; intensified economic boycott, the exclusion of Jews from government employment, public office or civil service, all tended to sap the courage and morale of Poland's more than 3,000,000 Jews.

Child care, feeding and training through the Centos, the Toz and various religious and cultural organizations, were among the most significant activities supported by the J. D. C. In tens of thousands of cases, children received their only hot meal of the day through the support of the J. D. C. Other thousands were trained in productive occupations, with the object of restratifying Poland's Jews along more normal occupational lines. Summer and winter colonies helped to better the health of underprivileged children; medical-sanitary work relieved countless cases of rickets, undernourishment and more serious ailments such as tuberculosis and cardiac diseases. Nor was medical aid restricted to youngsters alone. Pre- and post-natal clinics were established to guide Jewish mothers, and medical service was extended to needy adults. Sanitary service, particularly through the Toz, helped to raise the living standards of thousands of Jewish families, and helped to ward off the diseases spread by poverty and destitution.

Perhaps most important of all in the economic life of Poland's Jews was the network of Gemiloth Chesed kassas (free loan societies). These credit agencies formed the life-line of helpless Jews everywhere; with a small loan of $10 to

$20 furnished without interest charges, a small trader or artisan was able to tide over and to make both meager ends meet. The number of these kassas, which the J. D. C. had revitalized in 1926, grew steadily. By the end of 1933, 676 were functioning in Poland alone; five years later, in December of 1938, the number had increased to 915. This form of economic aid was supplemented by the cooperative credit kassas of the American Joint Reconstruction Foundation, which continued to make loans to small businessmen at a low interest rate.

The years 1935, 1936 and 1937 told the story of an heroic struggle. The Jews of Germany, with the help of their fellow Jews in other lands, attempted to rise above the series of calamities which had struck them. The Nuremberg Laws, spreading disorders, wholesale arrests, and above all, the tightening of the economic noose steadily dissipated their remaining hope. Almost every day brought a new decree, or a new interpretation of an old decree, which meant loss of employment for Jewish families. Jewish participation in cultural endeavors had long since been practically discontinued; now the only field open to Jews—commerce—was being rigidly narrowed. Emigration proceeded apace, even in the face of dwindling opportunities for entry to foreign countries. Those who could leave Germany did so, leaving behind them the bulk of their wealth.

By April 1, 1935, the Jews of Germany were able to achieve an unprecedented unification of communal activity. Economic relief, social welfare work, emigration and vocational retraining and all other communal activities which had been carried on up to that time largely and necessarily on an emergency basis, were reorganized along scientific and more orderly

46

lines. Practically all Jewish organizations of any consequence united within the framework of the Reichsvertretung der Juden in Deutschland and its operating agency, the Zentral Ausschuss, in order to cope more effectively with the special problems created by Nazi policies.

The Reichsvertretung established four committees for the conduct of its work—a committee on emigration, a committee on economic relief, a committee on social service problems and a committee on fund-raising. Local contributions were gathered to the full extent of the giving ability of Germany's Jews; they were supplemented by grants from foreign organizations, of which the J. D. C.'s contribution was generally larger than the aggregate of all other contributions from abroad.

From the very first, emigration statistics formed a barometer of Jewish conditions within Germany. After the initial outpouring which followed the accession to power of the National Socialist Party, emigration figures dropped considerably. But with the promulgation of the Nuremberg Laws in September of 1935, emigration received tremendous impetus and the figures began to rise.

The chief obstacles to large scale emigration were the rigid immigration laws of those countries offering the most likely prospects for permanent settlement. Generally it was easier for artisans and trained workers to find immigration opportunities than for merchants and professional men. As the European countries, still suffering from the economic depression, shut their doors more tightly than ever, Palestine, North and South America, and South Africa became the chief emigration centers.

As a corollary to the emigration movement, a system of

vocational retraining was developed. The Jews of Germany early discovered that no emigration on any considerable scale could succeed if the emigrants were not properly prepared for life in the new countries. Nor was retraining restricted only to preparation for emigration. Those Jews who could not leave for one reason or another, but who were nevertheless ousted from their professions and occupations, had to learn to earn their livelihood anew in those fields which were still open to Jewish employment.

Bitter as were the blows rained on German Jewish adults during these years, it was the children who were most severely affected. With heroic self-sacrifice, the leaders of German Jewry recognized that the children and the youth must first and foremost be given opportunity to develop into normal human beings and to live normal lives—if not in Germany, then elsewhere. Every effort was made to prevent the warping of young souls and the shattering of youthful ideals. Discrimination against Jewish children in schools was one of the earliest manifestations of National Socialism; this type of badgering developed from the setting aside of special "ghetto benches" in the classroom and the boycott of Jewish children by their non-Jewish playmates, to a decree, passed early in 1936, whereby Jewish children were forced to attend special Jewish schools. This decree confronted the Reichsvertretung with several knotty problems. An entire new Jewish educational system had to be built up. Facilities were not available for the absorption, in a single year, of the 20,000 Jewish children who attended general public schools. There were not enough Jewish teachers suitably trained to undertake this type of instruction. Textbooks, pamphlets and other necessary materials were lacking. Eventually, however, the transition was completed, and a Jewish school system was inaugurated to meet the needs of German Jewish children. Towards all of this work the J. D. C. made, and has continued to make, substantial contributions.

Until the year 1938, the legal process of eliminating Jews from the German economy was limited largely to public office holders, the professional classes—doctors, lawyers, teachers, artists, writers—and to some specific industries. Losses sustained by Jews in commerce and related fields were largely the result of boycotts and pressure methods of one sort or another. In order to reduce the losses from forced sales of businesses, the committee on economic relief of the Reichsvertretung set up a special fund in 1935, the loans from which enabled businessmen to save part of their capital. Similarly, special loans were also granted to prevent foreclosure of homes. The importance of this type of activity can be shown by the fact that during 1935, approximately 45 percent of the Jewish population of Germany sought the aid of the economic committees. A further major role in shoring up the crumbling structure of Jewish economy in Germany was played by the American Joint Reconstruction Foundation, which built up a cooperative loan kassa system in Germany similar to that which operates in East European countries.

While the Joint Distribution Committee and other foreign agencies assisted the German Jewish community in meeting the abnormal, extraordinary burdens imposed by their new problems, the normal needs of internal relief were considered primarily a local responsibility. To meet the ever increasing needs for domestic welfare work, the Jewish communities taxed themselves even beyond the limits of their capacities.

It was during 1936 that a distinguished British delegation visited the United States. From the discussions with this delegation emerged the formation of the Council for German

Jewry. The delegation placed before the Jewish groups in the United States a plan for enlarged emigration from Germany over a number of years together with projects for training and retraining; also proposals for the coordination of the efforts of the existing agencies concerned with bringing aid in the German Jewish situation.

Following a number of conferences with the British group, it was made clear that the J. D. C. would be glad to cooperate even more closely with the British Jews than theretofore and to make a substantial contribution toward the contemplated German emigration program, as it had been doing since the beginning of the crisis. On August 14, 1936, a statement was made public announcing the formation of the Executive Committee for the Council for German Jewry, representing the Jewish communities of the United States and Great Britain, for the purpose of assisting in the resettlement of Jews from Germany in other countries. The British section of the Council soon replaced the Central British Fund as the fund-raising body in Great Britain, and the J. D. C. has kept in closest touch with that organization.

A little earlier, there had been organized in the United States the Refugee Economic Corporation, with which was affiliated the Emigré Charitable Fund, Inc. The object of the Refugee Economic Corporation was the economic reconstruction and the settlement of refugees from Germany in other countries on a business, rather than purely philanthropic, basis. The Emigré Charitable Fund, Inc. was created in order to finance and supplement such activities as do not fall directly within the purview of the Corporation itself. Since its inception, the Refugee Economic Corporation has established a number of loan funds in the United States, Switzerland, Denmark, South Africa, the Argentine and Brazil. In addition, both the Refugee Economic Corporation and the Emigré Charitable Fund have helped to resettle refugees in agricultural colonies and in some instances provided training facilities to equip refugees for agricultural pursuits.

At the beginning of 1936, consideration had been given to the advisability of discontinuing the united fund-raising apparatus of the J. D. C. and the American Palestine Campaign, known as the United Jewish Appeal. By mutual consent, the J. D. C. and the Palestine group pursued separate fund-raising efforts. Thus it was that during 1936–37–38 separate fund-raising campaigns were conducted by the respective national offices of these organizations, although many welfare fund and other communities raised funds for both in locally centralized campaigns.

With the approach of the year 1938, the J. D. C. found itself facing a program whose needs were as ramified and intensive as those which had confronted the Jews of Europe during the tragic war and post-war days. Increased needs and spreading misery were foreseen. The budget adopted at the beginning of the year provided for a minimum expenditure of $5,100,000. It could not, of course, have anticipated or provided for the series of catastrophes that 1938 brought with it. Early in the year, the short-lived dictatorship of Octavian Goga in Rumania resulted in a reign of terror for that country's 900,000 Jews. Then, in March, there fell a crushing blow, the Anschluss of Austria with Germany. In one fell swoop, an additional 190,000 defenseless men, women and children were brought under the Nazi heel. In the course of a few weeks, the Jews of Austria were reduced to the same pitiful status as the Jews of Germany.

It quickly became all too clear that here was an emergency of huge proportions, where the J. D. C. would have to render

51

assistance without delay. In short order, machinery was set up to help the Jews of Austria. As in every other case, the J. D. C. operated through an established local agency, the Israelitische Kultusgemeinde in Vienna. A chain of soup kitchens was set up, and in the first few months after the Anschluss, more than $1,000 a day was being spent for feeding alone. An emigration office was established and retraining facilities instituted. The Anschluss swelled the tide of refugees to flood proportions. Thousands of Austrian Jews were pushed across borders, stateless and penniless. Hundreds were forced to swim rivers in the dead of night to reach neighboring countries. Truckload after truckload of unfortunate men, women and children was shipped across borders by Gestapo agents, there left to their miserable fate.

The absorption of Austria by Germany shocked the conscience of the world. President Franklin D. Roosevelt of the United States took the initiative, and within a few days after the Anschluss issued a memorable statement calling upon many Governments of the world to convene, in order to consider the plight of the refugees.

When the Intergovernmental Conference on Refugees assembled at Evian, France, in July, 1938, the J. D. C. was informally represented by a number of its officers and colleagues. A statement was presented, reviewing the work which the J. D. C. had done in behalf of refugees since the inception of the German crisis and tendering its wholehearted cooperation. That cooperation has been fulfilled and implemented since the Evian conference by the closest contact between J. D. C. and the Intergovernmental Refugee Bureau which was subsequently set up in London.

Almost every month during 1938 brought with it a new catastrophe. In May, 450,000 Jews in Hungary were subjected to a *numerus clausus,* reducing their participation in professional and business life to 20 percent of the total. Shortly thereafter, Italy announced that, in September, it would embark on a new racial policy whereby Jews would be denied the right to make a living. Even worse, some 15,000 foreign Jews who had taken up residence in Italy after 1919 were given six months in which to leave the country.

All of these events, shattering as they were, were but a prelude to developments in the fall. September saw the first partition of Czechoslovakia, with the annexation of the Sudeten area by Germany, the ceding of the Teschen district to Poland, and the surrender of sections of Slovakia to Hungary. As a result of the Munich Pact, 22,000 Jews who were former residents of the Sudeten areas became refugees from Germany. The word "no man's land" began to become a commonplace. All along the borders of former Czechoslovakia were isolated areas containing as many as 3,000 homeless, terrified Jews living under the most primitive conditions and unable to move either backwards or forwards.

In consequence of a disagreement between Poland and Germany caused by international strain, on October 30, more than 20,000 Polish Jews living in Germany were deported en masse and dumped over the border into Poland. The Polish deportations resulted in the creation of a huge "no man's land" sector at Zbaszyn. As a climax to this gruesome incident, there came a day early in November, when a half-crazed young refugee in Paris leveled a revolver at a German Embassy official. His pulling of the trigger was the pretext for a most unprecedented wave of violence and brutality. A huge pogrom in Germany set fire to hundreds of synagogues and caused the arrest of almost every able-bodied male Jew between the ages of 18 and 60.

It was against this background of violence and tragedy that the J. D. C. operated during 1938. It had to cope with overwhelming problems. It was called upon to render emergency assistance time and time again, and at the same time it dared not cease in its program of normal reconstructive aid.

VII. PRELUDE TO WAR, 1939

In the course of the year a number of welfare fund communities expressed their desire for more unified nationwide fund-raising. The J. D. C. entered into an agreement with the United Palestine Appeal once more to combine fund-raising efforts, and the United Jewish Appeal for Refugees and Overseas Needs was launched early in 1939 with a $20,000,000 goal. The third participant in the campaign was the National Coordinating Committee Fund, Inc. (later reorganized as the National Refugee Service, Inc.) which had assumed increasing importance and responsibilities because of the steady influx of German, Austrian and other refugees into the United States.

The new year brought no cessation in the troubles besetting the Jews of Europe. The early months of the year saw the second partition of Czechoslovakia, the occupation of Memel by Germany and the extension of anti-Semitic laws in Hungary, Rumania and Italy. With Austria, Memel and Sudetenland annexed by Germany, and with Bohemia, Moravia and Slovakia under German domination, a peculiar and tragic cycle was completed. In 1933 the Jewish population of Germany was 565,000. Now, despite the emigration of 350,000 Jews, the Jewish population of Greater Germany was 590,000. The pressure upon Jews to emigrate was tremendous and during the first nine months of the year the refugee problem became a primary task of those organizations seeking to help distressed Jewry. The emigrants of 1938–1939 were the poorest of all the refugees. The wealthier element had emigrated long before, and even those who had been comparatively well off in Germany had lost the bulk of their possessions as a result of the November decrees and were forced to leave their remaining assets in Germany. In view of the circumstances, most of the European countries were inclined to accord more favorable treatment to the refugees and made special concessions in emergency cases. Regulations were particularly eased in efforts to admit Jewish children from the Reich.

The main hope of the refugees for permanent settlement naturally centered in overseas countries, but the panicky flight which followed the pogroms of November 10, 1938, and the second partition of Czechoslovakia in March 1939, caused many of the Latin-American countries to bar their doors by demanding guarantees and head taxes, by stricter application of their normal regulations or by passing new restrictive immigration laws. Despite this, so great was the pressure, that refugees became the easy victims of unscrupulous steamship agents and officials. Frequently, refugees obtained inadequate or invalid documents from consuls in Europe that subsequently were not honored by the central governments represented by these officials. Sometimes regulations were changed while refugees were on the high seas and as a result whole boatloads of refugees wandered from land to land and port to port, seeking admission.

A shocking example of such a boatload of unfortunates, which focused the attention of the entire world upon this phase of the refugee problem, was the Hamburg-American liner *S.S. St. Louis* which sailed from Germany for Cuba on May 15, 1939. When the ship arrived in Cuba, 907 refugees on the boat were refused admittance on the basis that their landing permits, issued by the Cuban Commissioner of

Immigration, had been voided. Despite efforts by the National Coordinating Committee and the offer of the J. D. C. to put up a substantial cash bond if these refugees were admitted, the *St. Louis* passengers, after days of agonizing suspense, were forced to retrace their steps. As the ship started back toward Germany, the J. D. C. began efforts anew to find temporary havens for its passengers in Europe. The pleas of the J. D. C. and its cooperating agencies were accepted by the benevolent governments of England, France, Holland and Belgium and, under financial guarantees totaling $500,000 made by the J. D. C., the 907 refugees were admitted into these countries.

South America was not the only place on the globe where these wandering ships sought to land their human cargoes. Dozens of ships with thousands of refugees wandered in the Mediterranean trying to land their passengers along the Palestine coast, despite the restricted Palestine immigration schedule. When, as often happened, the ships were turned back, their luckless passengers were stranded in such remote places as the Greek Islands or Beirut.

With the spreading of the refugees to the four corners of the earth, the radius of operations of the J. D. C. naturally also spread from Europe to countries all over the world. During 1939 it was estimated that the J. D. C. operated in more than 50 countries. Funds were expended in such far-flung places as Bolivia, Shanghai, the Philippines, Cuba, Denmark, Iceland and Albania. Wherever refugees from Germany had gone, fleeing from terror and oppression, the J. D. C. followed, bringing with it the measure of assistance made possible by the generosity of American Jews.

In the meantime, the Intergovernmental Refugee Committee continued its efforts to regulate the flow of refugee emigration and to find permanent settlement opportunities. In July, 1939, there was announced the formation of a Coordinating Foundation which would implement plans for orderly large-scale emigration of Jews from Germany. At the request of representative Jewish personalities and organizations in the United States, the Joint Distribution Committee appropriated $1,000,000 as an underwriting toward the capital of the Co-ordinating Foundation.

VIII. THE J. D. C. TODAY

The political and other factors which brought so much misery to the refugees had even graver implications for Europe as a whole. International tension grew month by month during 1939. As war clouds gathered, the J. D. C. took steps to organize its affairs abroad so as to be able to render the maximum service wherever demands might arise. The number of American citizens on the staff abroad was increased and arrangements made to keep the lines of communication open insofar as possible. Substantial funds were appropriated to meet the initial stages of the need created by the war emergency.

Germany invaded Poland on September 1, and within two days Great Britain and France were at war with Germany. As the German war machine swept across Poland, the large Jewish population of that country was caught in its path. Whole villages and towns were destroyed and thousands of civilians, Jews and non-Jews alike, were killed or added to the refugee hordes. Within a week, as the German forces closed down upon Warsaw, all communication was cut off. For a period of nearly two months, no word was had from the office of the Joint Distribution Committee in Warsaw. Then, as news began to trickle through again, the world learned the dramatic story of how relief work was carried on by the J. D. C. staff throughout the siege of Warsaw with funds that had been sent into the country prior to the outbreak of hostilities; this, despite the fact that the J. D. C. Warsaw office had been wrecked by shells and one of the directors seriously injured. In other parts of Poland, J. D. C.-supported committees and organizations conducted relief work in the midst of the hostilities. Even in the sector occupied by Soviet Russia, emergency aid was rendered with J. D. C. funds.

In the meantime, relief efforts for war refugees were also organized by the J. D. C. in the countries bordering on Poland. Food, shelter, clothing and medical aid were provided for war sufferers who had fled into the Baltic countries and Rumania and Hungary.

Again confronted by world war, the J. D. C. recognized now, as in 1914–1918, that the problem transcended sectarian needs. The J. D. C. offered its facilities to the major American relief agencies such as the American Red Cross, the American Friends' Service Committee (Quakers) and the Commission for Polish Relief, to effect such cooperation and coordination as might be of the greatest benefit to all victims.

Thus, as the J. D. C. ended its twenty-fifth year, the wheel of time had completed a full turn. Once more the J. D. C. found itself facing problems similar to those which had brought about its establishment in 1914, but vastly magnified. In those twenty-five years, the J. D. C. had marshaled the resources of the Jews of America and directed a steady stream of life-giving assistance overseas. It had saved hundreds of thousands of lives and enabled countless others to rehabilitate themselves.

Intertwined in the twenty-five year background of the J. D. C. are the threads of the history not only of the Jews of Central and Eastern Europe—their trials, their problems, their efforts and their hopes—but also of the Jews of America.

The quarter century was one of splendid achievement in American Jewish life. It saw the rise to pre-eminence in the public service, as in the cause of our fellow Jews, of a number of Jewish families. In the history of the J. D. C. there may be found the expression of the tradition of service, carried from father to son. The late Julius Rosenwald was a moving spirit at the inception of the J. D. C. and throughout many years. Today his son, William Rosenwald, is a vice-chairman of the J. D. C. and all the other members of his family continue to give evidence of their devotion to this work. The late Felix M. Warburg was perhaps the greatest single influence in shaping the destinies of the J. D. C. Today his son, Edward M. M. Warburg, is a vice-chairman. James Marshall, son of the late Louis Marshall, is a member of the Executive Committee. The Lehman family has been represented since the earliest days of the Committee, by the late Arthur Lehman as well as by Herbert H. Lehman, the distinguished Governor of the State of New York, who is today the senior vice-chairman of the J. D. C. Pauline Baerwald Falk, daughter of the J. D. C.'s present chairman, organized and heads the J. D. C. Junior Division.

The present officers of the J. D. C. represent an interesting admixture of the older generation and the younger. Younger men are eagerly training themselves for enlarged service under the tutelage of wise and seasoned statesmen and philanthropists. The present officers of the J. D. C. are: Mrs. Felix M. Warburg, honorary chairman; Paul Baerwald, chairman; Herbert H. Lehman, James N. Rosenberg, George Backer, James H. Becker, David M. Bressler, Alexander Kahn, William Rosenwald, Edward M. M. Warburg and Jonah B. Wise, vice-chairmen; Marco F. Hellman and I. Edwin Goldwasser, treasurers; William A. Koshland, associate treasurer; Miss Evelyn M. Morrissey, assistant treasurer; Mrs. H. B. L. Goldstein, comptroller; Joseph C. Hyman, secretary and executive director; Joseph J. Schwartz, assistant secretary; Isidor Coons, campaign director; James N. Rosenberg, chairman, National Council; Dr. Bernhard Kahn, honorary chairman, European Executive Council; and Morris C. Troper, chairman, European Executive Council.

As presently constituted, the J. D. C. has the following active sub-committees: Administration Committee, Edward M. M. Warburg, chairman; Organization Committee, James H. Becker, chairman; Budget and Scope Committee, David M. Bressler, chairman; Committee on Program of Aid in Poland and Eastern European Countries, Alexander Kahn, chairman; Committee on Program of Aid in European Countries of Refuge, Edward M. M. Warburg, chairman; Committee on Program of Aid in Central and South America, Alfred Jaretzki, Jr., chairman; Cultural Committee, Dr. Cyrus Adler, chairman; Publicity Committee, George Backer and Harold K. Guinzburg, co-chairmen; Campaign Committee, Rabbi Jonah B. Wise, chairman; and Committee on Personnel, Mrs. H. B. L. Goldstein, chairman.

Space does not permit listing the names of the large group of men and women who both in the United States and Europe have served the cause of overseas Jewry, nor is it possible to name the many devoted workers and directors in the J. D. C. offices here as well as in the campaigns throughout the country.

Herbert Hoover, observing the work of the J. D. C., as long ago as 1923, remarked that "there is no brighter chapter in the whole history of philanthropy than that which could be written of the work of the American Jews in the last nine years."

Now those years are nearly three times nine, many of them as black as any in Jewish history, but fortunately American Jews have not abruptly closed that bright chapter of philanthropy, and its last pages have yet to be written.